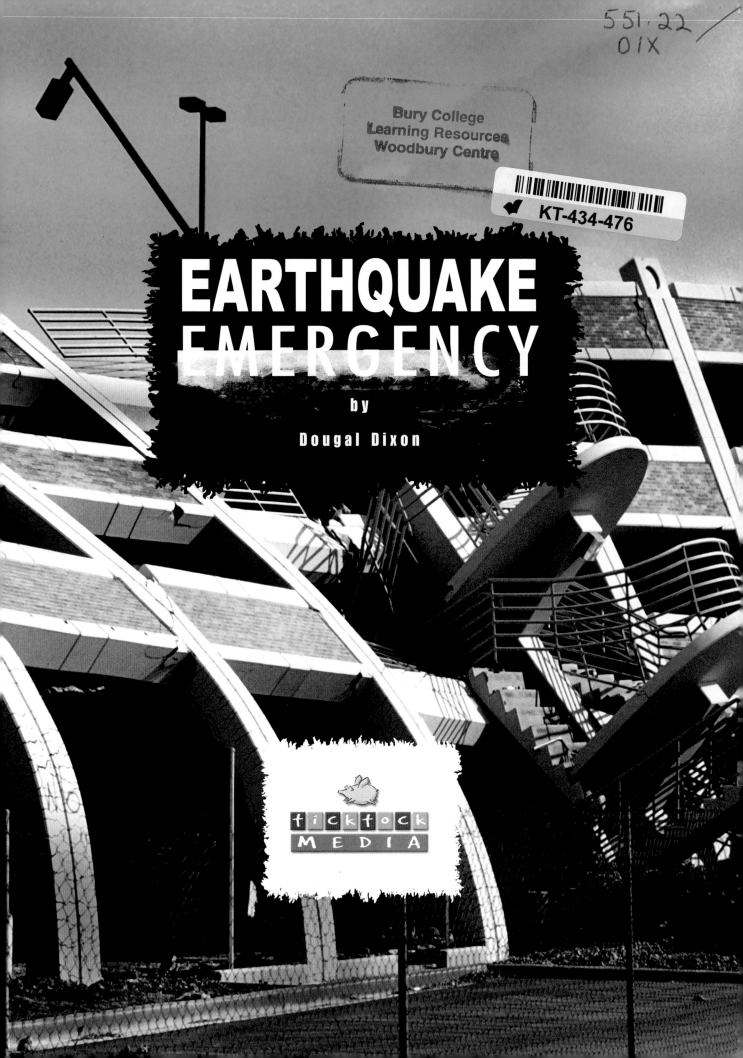

EARTHQUAKE
EMERGENCY

by

Dougal Dixon

ticktock
MEDIA

EXPEDITION EARTH

EARTHQUAKE EMERGENCY

by Dougal Dixon

Copyright © ticktock Entertainment Ltd 2004

First published in Great Britain in 2004 by ticktock Media Ltd.,

Unit 2, Orchard Business Centre, North Farm Road, Tunbridge Wells, Kent, TN2 3XF

We would like to thank: David Gillingwater and Elizabeth Wiggans

Illustrations by John Alston and David Gillingwater

ISBN 1-57768-438-3 hbk

ISBN 1-57768-434-0 pbk

A CIP catalogue record for this book is available from the British Library.

t=top, b=bottom, c=center, l=left, r=right, OFC=outside front cover, OBC=outside back cover

Alamy: 10-11c. Corbis: 12-13c, 16-17c, 22-23c, 24-25c, 28-29c, Creatas: 20-21.

Every effort has been made to trace the copyright holders, and we apologize in advance for any unintentional omissions.
We would be pleased to insert the appropriate acknowledgements in any subsequent edition of this publication.

Printed in China

CONTENTS

DAY 1

Location: *Media Room, City School*

Louise Grove

Hi! I am Louise Grove. I have always been interested in earthquakes and their incredible destructive power. At the moment I am writing a feature about earthquakes for my school project.

This summer I am staying with my friend Tasos on an island in the eastern Mediterranean. The area is very prone to earthquakes. Looks like I am in the perfect place to do my research! Last night, Tasos's uncle, a doctor at the local earthquake observatory dropped by. He said he'd heard about my project, and wondered if I'd like to come up to the observatory tomorrow and take a look. I can hardly wait!

There have been so many films about earthquakes on television recently, however, that I don't really think I want to experience one first hand...

Greetings from the local castle. Built in the 12th century, it has X-shaped cracks in the brickwork, which is a sign that it has been hit by earthquakes in the past.

The castle's local name is *Ochok*, which means "island" in the local language. The castle is now on a peninsula but it may have been an island at one time. This shows that the coastline is changing - maybe because of the effect of earthquakes.

If you look at the map of the island below, you can see that all the mountains, ridges, and peninsulas stretch from east to west. (This means that there is likely stress between the rock plates in that direction.)

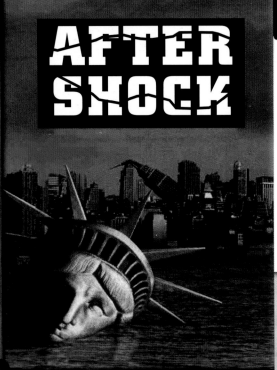

This is a poster from my favorite film, *After Shock*. It is about an earthquake that strikes the United States.

Upper Town

New airport

Plateau

Observatory

Ocheck Castle

Old airport

Lower Town

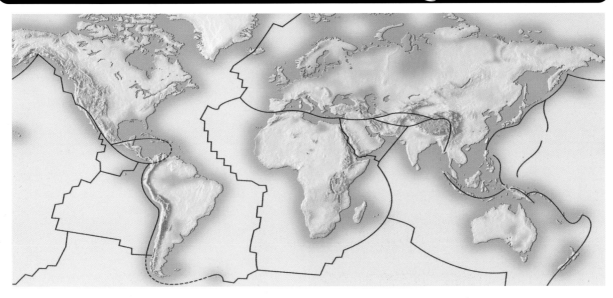

Why do earthquakes happen? Researchers theorise that the outer shell, or *lithosphere*, of the earth, is made up of a number of separate plates, called *tectonic plates*. These plates fit together like pieces of a jigsaw puzzle. Scientists think that there are seven large plates and several smaller ones. According to current research, earthquakes occur along plate boundaries when crustal plates move against each other. Scientists call the crack that occurs between these plates a *fault*.

EARTHQUAKES

The Mediterranean sea lies along a boundary between plates. The African plate is sliding eastwards in relation to the European. The map shows the north-south rift valleys where Europe is being stretched, and S-shaped bends in mountain chains. All this movement is accompanied by earthquakes.

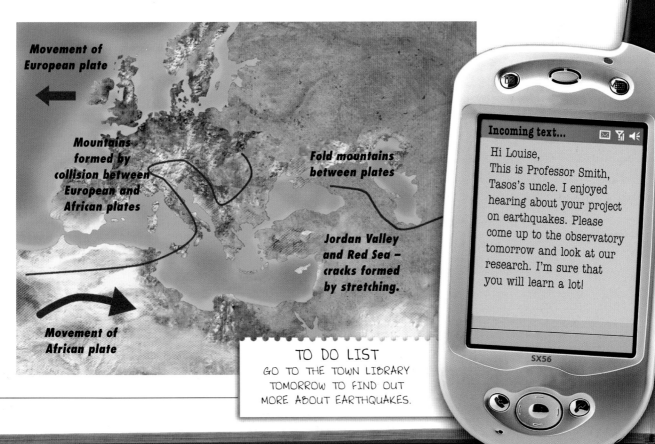

Movement of European plate

Mountains formed by collision between European and African plates

Fold mountains between plates

Jordan Valley and Red Sea – cracks formed by stretching.

Movement of African plate

Incoming text...

Hi Louise,
This is Professor Smith, Tasos's uncle. I enjoyed hearing about your project on earthquakes. Please come up to the observatory tomorrow and look at our research. I'm sure that you will learn a lot!

SX56

TO DO LIST
GO TO THE TOWN LIBRARY
TOMORROW TO FIND OUT
MORE ABOUT EARTHQUAKES.

DAY 2
Location: *Town Library*

I think I had better look into the history of earthquakes before I visit the Doctor at the observatory.

One of the biggest earthquakes in the last century was the one that took place in Tangshan in China, in 1976. During the night of 28 July a loud bang was heard, and the ground began to shake rapidly. The first vibrations were quite small, but then huge areas of land started to swirl about in a twisting motion and violent jolts were felt. The whole earthquake only took about ten seconds but in that time the city was reduced to rubble. The earthquake had a magnitude of 8.3 on the Richter scale, making it one of the strongest on record. Had such a thing happened in an unpopulated area the damage would have been slight, but here it happened in one of the most important industrial centres of the country.

Tangshan was so devastated by the earthquake that it took ten years to repair the damage.

TANGSHAN DEVASTATED BY EARTHQUAKE

Over 650,000 buildings collapsed in Tangshan – about 90 percent of the city. Almost a quarter of a million people, or a tenth of the population, died. Help was slow to arrive because the earthquake destroyed railway tracks and roads. Radio station were knocked out as well. It took several hours for Bejing, the country's capital, to learn about the earthquake.

Taken from *The Shaker*, July 29, 1976

The cause of the Tangshan earthquake was a deep geological fault about 7 miles directly below the city.

Great Wall of China

CHINA

Haicheng

Beijing

Tangshan

KOREA

TOWN LIBRARY
Louise Grove
STUDENT

13515521 243

Streets were ripped apart by the power of the earthquake's vibrations.

Houses everywhere were reduced to rubble by the vibrations

SORTING OUT THE PROBLEM

Once the government of China received news of the disaster, it quickly mobilized people to help. Over 100,000 workers arrived in Tangshan to offer help. They built 370,000 homes before the onset of the severe Chinese winter.

Taken from *The Shaker,* July 31, 1976

TANGSHAN RECOVERS

The Chinese government wanted people to forget the tragedy of the disaster. When the railway line through the city was rebuilt, walls were erected to hide the view of the ruins from the eyes of travelers.

Taken from *The Shaker,* September 1, 1977

DAY 3
Location: *Town Library*

Japan is used to earthquakes. They happen all the time, because the island chain is on the "ring of fire" – the plate boundary that surrounds the Pacific Ocean. However the country was unprepared for the 7.2 magnitude quake that struck the major city of Kobe at 5.46 in the mornng on 17 January 1995. The earthquake lasted about 20 seconds and opened up the strait between Kobe and an offshore island by about two metres and pushed the city over a metre upwards.

The old wooden buildings caught fire easily, fuelled by gas from ruptured pipes, and the fires were difficult to control because the water mains were put out of action. Over 240 individual fires broke out, and they burned for 24 hours.

Kobe was one of the most important seaports in Japan, handling 30 per cent of the container trade. Nearly all the shipping berths were totally destroyed.

The disaster cost Japan 0.2 per cent of its GNP and caused great disruption to the country's international trade.

A City in Ruins

Most of Kobe's modern buildings survived, but 65,000 older houses were destroyed.

CHILDREN PRACTICE EARTHQUAKE DRILL

In Japan, every school holds earthquake drills. Ever since a catastrophic earthquake devastated the capital of Tokyo in 1923, the city has held an annual earthquake day. On the anniversary of the earthquake, everyone spends an entire day performing rescue and escape drills.

Taken from *The Shaker*, February 21, 1976

DESPERATE SURVIVORS

About 5,500 were killed in the Kobe earthquake and 36,500 were injured.

Bury College
Learning Resources
Woodbury Centre

Taken from *The Shaker*,
January 20, 1976

BRIDGE FALLS TO
POWER OF EARTHQUAKE
The most famous image of the Kobe earthquake
is of the raised Hansin expressway. Its concrete
supports collapsed, sending it toppling on its side.
At that time of the morning, the highway was almost deserted,
but two hours later it would have been filled with cars and trucks.

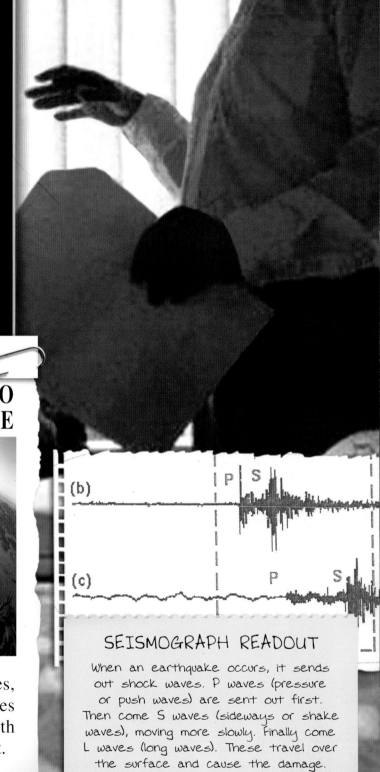

DAY 4
Location: *Earthquake Observatory*

I have just been up to the earthquake observatory. Wow! What a place. There are all sorts of instruments here that are used to try to monitor if there is an earthquake brewing.

It seems that there has not been an earthquake on the island for about fifty years. You would think that this is a good sign, but it is not. If a place in an earthquake zone has not had an earthquake for a long time it means that the stresses are building up. Finally the rocks will give way and the later that this happens then the bigger the resulting earthquake will be.

The main instrument here is a seismograph. When an earthquake occurs the seismograph picks up the shock waves that it sends out and produces a printout. This helps the seismologists tell the magnitude of the earthquake and the distance from its focus.

Taken from *The Shaker*, August 1, 2003

RESIDENTS OF SAN FRANCISCO ANXIOUSLY AWAIT NEXT 'QUAKE

California is prone to earthquakes, because the Pacific plate moves northward in relation to the North American plate along the San Andreas Fault.

SEISMOGRAPH READOUT

When an earthquake occurs, it sends out shock waves. P waves (pressure or push waves) are sent out first. Then come S waves (sideways or shake waves), moving more slowly. Finally come L waves (long waves). These travel over the surface and cause the damage.

(b)

(c)

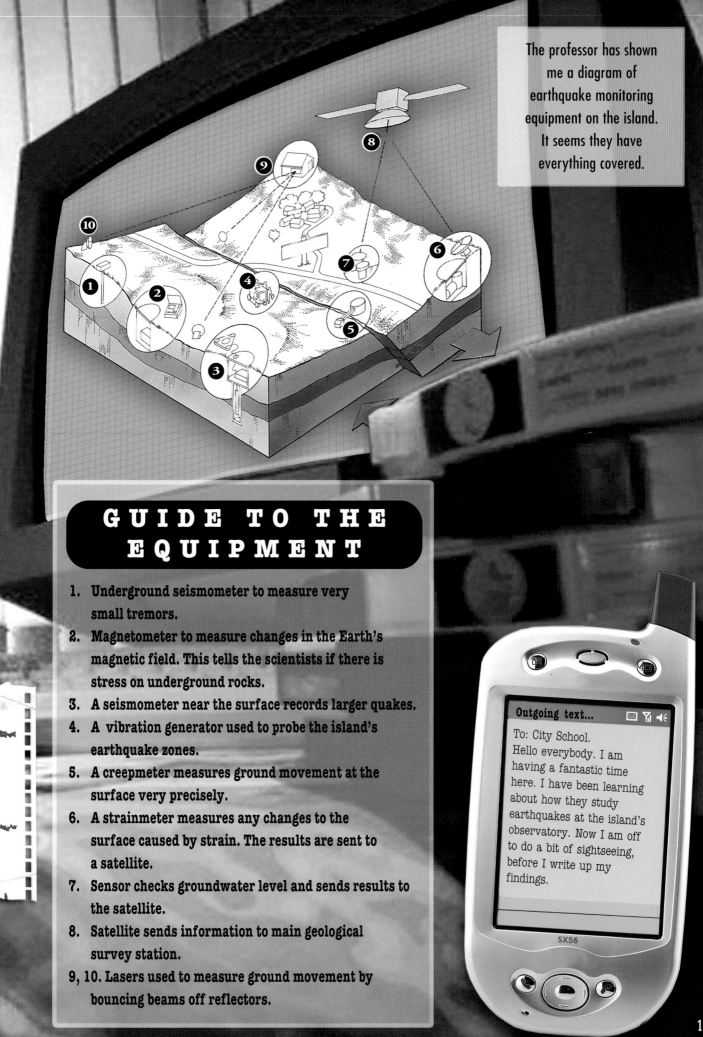

The professor has shown me a diagram of earthquake monitoring equipment on the island. It seems they have everything covered.

GUIDE TO THE EQUIPMENT

1. Underground seismometer to measure very small tremors.
2. Magnetometer to measure changes in the Earth's magnetic field. This tells the scientists if there is stress on underground rocks.
3. A seismometer near the surface records larger quakes.
4. A vibration generator used to probe the island's earthquake zones.
5. A creepmeter measures ground movement at the surface very precisely.
6. A strainmeter measures any changes to the surface caused by strain. The results are sent to a satellite.
7. Sensor checks groundwater level and sends results to the satellite.
8. Satellite sends information to main geological survey station.
9, 10. Lasers used to measure ground movement by bouncing beams off reflectors.

Outgoing text...

To: City School.
Hello everybody. I am having a fantastic time here. I have been learning about how they study earthquakes at the island's observatory. Now I am off to do a bit of sightseeing, before I write up my findings.

SX56

DAY 5
Location: *Near the Coast*

I have been trying to relax near the beach today, but I met a local fisherman who is very uneasy. He showed me a photograph that he took last night, of a strange red glow in the sky. He says that this only happens before an earthquake.

It seems that all the water drained out of his well during the past few days, and fish have been jumping out of his pond, which he claims are signs of an impending earthquake. And his dog barked all night, which it does not usually do.

I saw a big snake this morning. The receptionist at the hotel said that this was very unusual at this time of the year as they do not come out from under stones.

Up at the observatory, the Doctor told me that there are all sorts of things that may warn us of earthquakes, but the seismologists do not understand them yet, and there is no way of measuring them.

STRANGE GOINGS-ON
Animals are behaving strangely today. Farm animals like goats are fidgety. Birds are migrating at the wrong time of the year. Maybe they feel that something is wrong.

INFORMATION FROM THE SKIES

Yesterday the professor showed me this satellite image of the island. The red and yellow patches indicate an increase in infrared emissions along the main fault line of the island. (Infrared omissions indicate heat.) Could this mean the island is in danger of a quake?

EARTHQUAKE SAFETY TIPS

In the event of an earthquake, you should take the following precautions:

1. Take cover immediately under a sturdy table or desk, cover your eyes with your arm, and hold on tightly to something secure.
2. If there is no table or desk in the room, sit on the floor against an inside wall away from windows, bookcases, or furniture that could fall on you.
3. Do not go to another room. Always stay inside until the shaking stops and you are sure it is safe to exit.
4. If you are outside when a quake begins, move away from buildings, trees, and power lines. Drop to the ground.
5. If you are in a car, slow down and drive to a place away from power lines, buildings, and trees. Stay in the car.
6. Expect aftershocks after the earthquake stops. Each time one occurs, follow the same precautions as outlined above.

A Fault Through the Island
There are two major faults that run through the island. Most of the strange occurrences have been observed near Fault 2. The professor says if anything is going to happen, it will happen here.

Fault 1

Fault 2

Farms report loss of water from wells

Lights seen in northern sky

DAY 6
Location: *Main Street, Lower Town*

Just look at this town! Obviously the builders do not bother with earthquake-proofing houses when there has been no major earthquake in living memory. The island is not a rich place and so it has never been able to afford to implement anti-earthquake measures. Now the economy is on an upturn because of tourist revenue and something may be done about it. But not yet!

At the other side of the island, Upper Town has regular earthquake drills, but this is a modern phenomenon. The place is no more earthquake proof than Lower Town.

From what I heard from the locals yesterday I am beginning to worry. They seem to believe that an earthquake is coming. If a big earthquake hits this town, the old buildings will crumble, the brickwork will crack, and more modern structures will probably sink into mud.

The professor handed me this report from a local firm of architects. We better hope an earthquake doesn't hit us or there will be trouble.

ARCHITECT'S REPORT:
TOWN NOT READY FOR QUAKES

The architecture of Lower Town has not accommodated the fact that this is a dangerous earthquake area. It consists of the usual Mediterranean whitewashed adobe houses stacked up on a hillside. Modern buildings are more substantially built but have overhanging balconies.

The professor is also an artist and did this quick watercolor of the town. It looks very pretty, but vulnerable to damage from earthquakes.

DISASTER IN SPITAK

The town of Spitak in Armenia has been flattened by a 6.9 magnitude earthquake. Armenia is such an impoverished country that it could not afford to build earthquake-proof buildings, despite the fact that it is in an earthquake zone. The death toll was about 100,000. Most of the deaths occurred when people were crushed by falling buildings.

Taken from *The Shaker*, July 12, 1988

Outgoing text...

To City School,
Suddenly I feel very uneasy about being here. The more I look at the buildings, the more I can imagine them falling down in an earthquake. Please, could everybody back home keep their fingers crossed for me?

SX56

CATASTROPHE!

DAY 7
Location: *Police Station, Lower Town*

Unfortunately my fears were right, and the worst thing could have happened to Lower Town has happened!

At 11.47 this morning everything began to shake. I was in the lobby of the hotel when it started. At first I thought it was one of the trams going by, but then the pictures started falling off the walls, and the walls themselves started to lean. I rushed out into the open, just as the ceiling crashed and a blast of dust and rubble followed me out of the front door. Then I saw that the surface of the street was rolling like sea waves. The tall buildings began shaking and brick walls were crumbling all around me. The shaking was so great that trams toppled off their tracks. A series of cracks, parallel to one another opened up in the cobbled road. Trees in a garden opposite were swaying back and forth. I could not stand up. This could not have lasted more than a few seconds, but it seemed like hours.

I took refuge in the police station. Much of the town centre was covered by security cameras, and we had a view of the different bits of devastation that occurred.

The fire service was immediately called into action

Paving slabs have been torn from their foundations

COAST TOWNS VULNERABLE TO QUAKES

Coastal towns located near fault lines are especially prone to earthquakes. On Cyprus in 365 A.D., a quake killed thousands. Archaeologists have found evidence of the quake. They have discovered skeletons, pots, vases, and other artifacts, including priceless mosaics.

I fished out this article that I picked up from the Town Library. It looks like we are experiencing a similar event.

Concrete buildings have collapsed because of the waves

Some areas will be contaminated with chemicals or sewage

Cars were swept into the harbour by the force of the earthquake

Tram lines have been twisted into strange shapes

People are moving around, either dazed or in a panic

Lower Town's water mains have burst.

DAY 7 – Afternoon
Location: *Lower Town boulevard*

The results are just as I feared.

The old town houses crumbled to dust. Sturdier brick walls broke up in X-shaped cracks and fell out into the street. The modern block of flats at the top of the town collapsed upon itself, each floor flattening the one below. Modern bungalows remained whole, but sank into liquefied mud. Cornices and balconies fell into the road. Soil became a slurry and flowed downhill. The smaller houses up the hillside are gone in a landslide – either buried or carried away. Water mains burst, sending water fountaining everywhere. Fires broke out all over the town, because many families were cooking lunch at the time. Flyovers collapsed. Tramlines are all twisted. The ground is all cracked open – the cracks seeming to follow the deformation of the tram lines.

I can't see this town ever getting back to normal. I am going down to the beach to get away from all this.

You can see the forces at work from the damage they cause. The direction of the first shock is shown by the direction in which the bridge toppled. The cracks in the road show how the blocks of the earth have moved.

I did ths sketch of the chaos that surrounds us. When you compare this drawing to the painting the Doctor did, you can see just how the town has been devastated.

It is obvious that the buildings were not constructed with earthquakes in mind.

Emergency services have been mobilized, but they have a big job ahead of them.

TSUNAMI!

DAY 7 – Afternoon
Location: *Close to the beach*

Many survivors gathered on the beach, mistakenly thinking they were safe there. Then word went around that the water had withdrawn from the shoreline – like the tide going out in a few minutes. This brought even more people down, to see what was happening.

Then the wave hit. It was a tsunami – what journalists call a "tidal wave." The main movement of the earthquake has disturbed the seafloor nearby, and this set up a huge sea wave. The water pulled back from the beach just to build up into a surge that has swept along the coastal esplanade of the town. I managed to leave the seafront and keep running. Tsunamis do not always come as single waves. Often they withdraw and attack again and again. As if the earthquake itself did not cause enough damage!

Word is coming in of even more damage across the island. I am dreading what the Doctor and his team are going to find...

Newsflash! Island's Airport Washed into Sea

During this morning's earthquake, the soil beneath the runways of the new airport along the coast became liquid because of the shaking caused by the earthquake. Because the airport was built on a slight slope, it slid down into the sea.

UNDERSTANDING TSUNAMIS

In wide-open oceans like the Pacific, people can prepare for tsunamis. After the Valdavia earthquake in Chile in 1961, seismologists could estimate the time it would take for the resulting tsunami to cross the Pacific Ocean. The map here indicates the number of hours it took for the tsunami to reach different parts of the Pacific. In an enclosed sea like the Mediterranean, there is not enough time for such warnings.

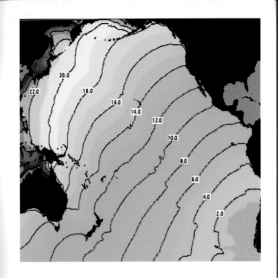

ANCHORAGE SHAKEN TO ITS CORE

Much of the damage to buildings during the Anchorage earthquake in Alaska happened because homes slid into the ground. The ground itself turned to a liquid form and would not support any structures.

Taken from *The Shaker*, March 28, 1964

Outgoing text...

Professor,
I just thought I'd let you know I am all right. I have survived the earthquake. I am going to make my way up to the observatory to see what you have found out about it.

SX56

DAY 7 - Evening
Location: *An old hall in Lower Town*

The rescue workers have begun to move in.

At least the country has a workable infrastructure for dealing with such an emergency. Many of the hospitals are still functioning.

UNESCO and the Department of Humanitarian Affairs of the United Nations have helped to set up a response. They are flying in medical staff from all over the world. Much of this has not kicked in yet, but the immediate humanitarian relief will be here soon.

More of a problem will be the long term effects. Traditionally both towns relied on fishing, olive growing and vineyards for its economy. In more recent years they have become tourist resorts. Now I have seen olive groves and vineyards swept down hillsides or buried, and the fishing wharves, at least at Lower Town, are ruined. Also, who wants to come to an earthquake-prone area for a holiday? It will be along time before this island is back to normal.

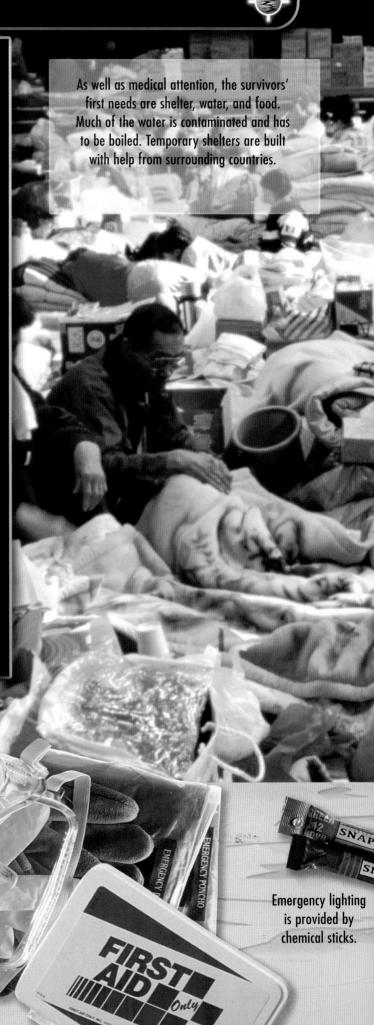

As well as medical attention, the survivors' first needs are shelter, water, and food. Much of the water is contaminated and has to be boiled. Temporary shelters are built with help from surrounding countries.

Rescue workers wear sterile gloves and goggles to help prevent the spread of disease.

They distribute first aid kits to the residents.

Emergency lighting is provided by chemical sticks.

A hospital ship is anchored just offshore from Lower Town. It can provide extra facilities for the island's injured.

烏龍茶

Blankets are an important component in the rescue equipment.

Outgoing text...

I don't think I can do much more work here. I feel I am getting in the way of the emergency services. Can I come up to the observatory and see what you have discovered about the earthquake?

SX56

Packs of concentrated food are being shipped in for survivors.

Bury College
Lear   ources
V

Simple things, such as pocket knives and flashlights are surprisingly useful.

WHERE THE BREAK OCCURRED

DAY 8
Location: *Ruins of the Capital*

I made it back to the observatory. The scientists are all working hard to determine where the main part of the earthquake occurred.

It seems that the epicentre was on the main fault at the western end of the island. I didn't know it but the 'epicentre' is not the point at which the earthquake originates. That is called the 'focus,' and is usually deep underground. The epicentre is the point on the surface directly above the focus. Usually the epicentre is the place where most damage is done, but for some reason Lower Town, on the south coast, seems to have suffered most during today's earthquake.

The Doctor tells me he can pinpoint the epicentre using P and S earthquake waves. These travel at different speeds and arrive at an observatory at different times. The gap between them tells how far away the focus is, so the focus must be on a circle of known radius. Compare the circles from three observatories and where they overlap, there is the focus, and hence the epicentre.

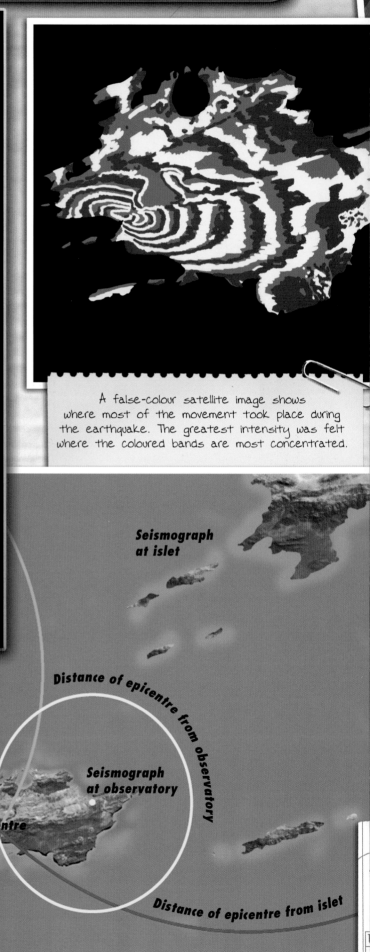

A false-colour satellite image shows where most of the movement took place during the earthquake. The greatest intensity was felt where the coloured bands are most concentrated.

Seismograph at islet

Distance of epicentre from observatory

Seismograph at observatory

Seismograph at lighthouse

N

Epicentre

Distance of epicentre from lighthouse

Distance of epicentre from islet

24

At the epicentre, a long, narrow crack called the *primary fissure* shows the main movement that has taken place. This represents the movement of the actual fault along which the rocks moved.

A seismograph prints out the reading of an earthquake on a long roll of paper. The first shock waves to arrive are P waves and the second are S waves. They travel at different speeds. The distance between them on the paper shows the interval between their times of arrival at the observatory. That interval tells scientists how far away the earthquake is.

P   S

P   S

(b)   P S

(c)   P   S

DAY 9
Location: *Observatory*

We are not done yet! As soon as I stepped into the observatory this morning the whole place began to sway. I thought I was just becoming dizzy from the excitement of the last two days, but the place really was moving. The Doctor said that it was an aftershock, not nearly as strong as the first. It seems we should expect a few of those over the next few days as the rocks of the island settle down. The jump produced by the initial shock usually moves the rocks too far, and aftershocks jostle them back into position.

The seismologists are now beginning to put together a picture of what actually happened on the island two days ago. It seems that the main shock had a magnitude of 5.0 on the Richter scale. This is a measure of the actual energy released. It was quite a big one.

The earthquake waves were halted by a massive fault at the south end of the island.

IV

low intensity this side of fault 1

fault 1

IX

VIII

fault 2

granite area more resistant to the earthquake

focus-point at which the earthquake occurs

MEXICO CITY IN RUINS

Mexico City has been ruined by an earthquake, even though it lies 250 miles from the earthquake's epicentre on the west coast of Mexico. The capital was built on a plain with soft sediments underneath. These sediments magnified the earthquake waves as they passed through them. This caused much greater damage in Mexico City than in the areas around it.

When a city is built on soft sediments, earthquakes cause disaster. This happened to Mexico City in 1985.

Taken from *The Shaker*, September 20, 1985

There are two main faults across the island. The movement took place along fault 2. The magnitude of the earthquake is measured on the Richter scale, from 1 to 10. The Doctor says that each number on the scale represents a 10-times increase in the ground movement recorded. So in an earthquake of magnitude 7, the ground moves nearly 100 times as much as in a quake of magnitude 5. The earthquake that hit our island measured a 6!

Professor Smith tells me that the intensity of an earthquake is measured on a different scale from the Richter scale and ranges from I, hardly noticeable, to XII, causing total devastation.

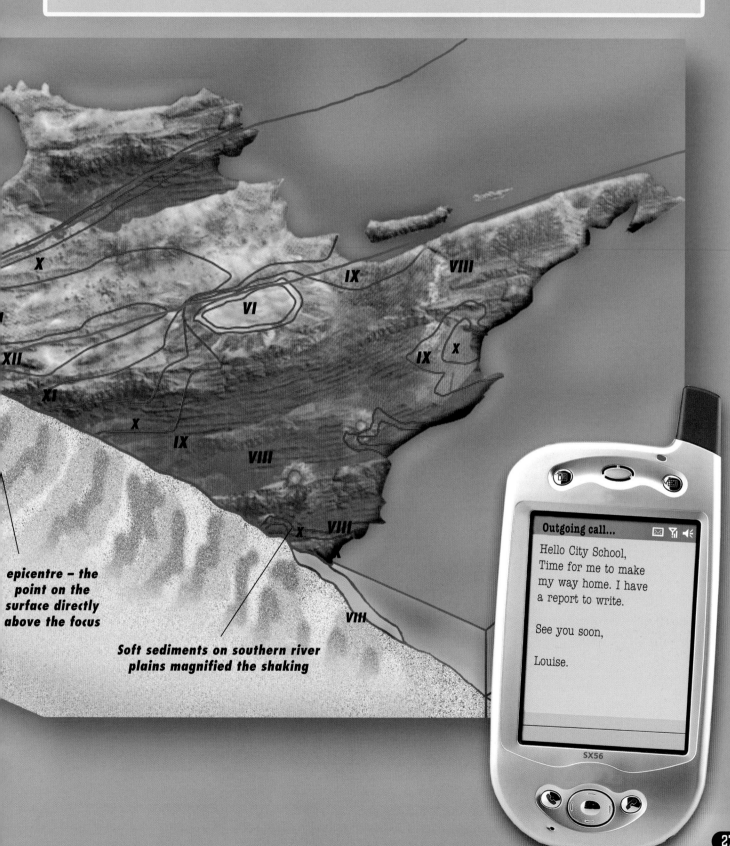

epicentre – the point on the surface directly above the focus

Soft sediments on southern river plains magnified the shaking

Outgoing call...

Hello City School,
Time for me to make
my way home. I have
a report to write.

See you soon,

Louise.

SX56

Here it is! My report on the earthquake disaster was published in our local paper.

A TOWN RECOVERS

A look at the Mediterranean island that was hit by a massive earthquake last year. With a special report by our junior reporter from the City School, Louise Grove.

There are two aspects to living through an earthquake – the scientific aspect and the human one.

On one level, it is fascinating to see the great movements of the earth at work, to actually witness the forces that shape our planet, that account for the positions of the continents and the distribution of mountains. It gives an appreciation of how our world came to be.

On the other hand, it is horrible to witness the pain and suffering that these forces cause. People seem so vulnerable compared with the motions of the earth.

Much research is now being done to try to understand the forces and to lessen the misery that they cause.

The traditional building materials in earthquake-prone Japan are bamboo and paper. Walls made of these materials cause little damage when they fall and can be replaced

Ancient monuments on the island have been protected with rubber and steel pads. These act as shock absorbers in the event of an earthquake.

Banks of seismographs monitor each tremor.

easily. But, modern buildings require stronger materials, and specialized building techniques must be used.

The National Centre for Earthquake Engineering and Research at New York State University in Buffalo is one of the leaders in this field. They have designed a shake table that mimics the forces produced by an earthquake, and they study building techniques using scale models. One of their discoveries is that a tall building has a particular resonance, like a pendulum. If an earthquake hits it at just the right frequency the shaking magnifies. This is what happened in Mexico City, where buildings higher than five stories but lower than 15 suffered the greatest damage.

One possible way of dealing with this could be by suspending a giant pendulum in a tall building. Once an earthquake is detected, the pendulum would be set swinging to counteract the natural swing of the building. Giant pistons could also be installed to produce the same effect. Rubber cushions could be incorporated between floors so that each floor becomes isolated from the other. That way, the building is not just one dangerously rigid structure.

New materials are being developed that absorb vibrations by bending and twisting rather than breaking. Brickwork can be stabilized by being encased in wire mesh.

The problem with all these techniques – experimental and established – is that they are all expensive. Builders must weigh the expense of such building materials against the likelihood of an

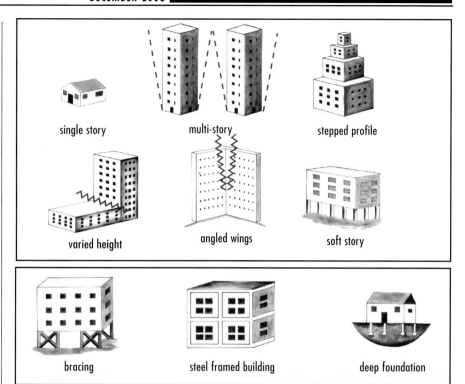

single story — multi-story — stepped profile

varied height — angled wings — soft story

bracing — steel framed building — deep foundation

The buildings above are all designed to be earthquake-proof. This means they have the best possible chance of surviving an earthquake.

earthquake occurring. It is too late for the people of the island, who suffered this time around. Perhaps when the towns are rebuilt using new technology, the island will be a safer place.

The island's observatory has been upgraded to make sure the community has the best possible chance of detecting earthquakes at the first opportunity.

GLOSSARY

Aftershock A smaller earthquake that often follows a big one. After the main shock the rocks have usually jumped too far and are still unstable. Aftershocks are felt as the rocks settle into a more stable position.

Department of Humanitarian Affairs The department of the United Nations that deals with the welfare of people all around the world.

Epicentre The point on the earth's surface directly above the focus of an earthquake. The epicentre is usually the site where the greatest damage occurs.

Esplanade A promenade by the sea.

Evacuate To move people away from a dangerous area

Fault In geology, a crack in the crust of the earth where there has been some movement. This movement usually takes place in the form of an earthquake.

Focus The point at which the greatest movement takes place during an earthquake. The focus is usually deep below the earth's surface, and usually lies on a fault. The point on the surface directly above is called the epicentre.

Harmonic When two pendulums are swinging, if they are swinging at exactly the same rate they are said to be in resonance. If they are swinging so that the rate of one is a multiple of the rate of the other they are in harmony. The harmonic is the rate of the swing of one compared to that of the other.

Infrastructure Basic components of a community, such as roads, power plants, transportation, and communication systems.

Intensity In an earthquake, the amount of disturbance produced at a particular place. The intensity of an earthquake is measured on the Mercalli scale that goes from I to XII. I represents movement that is felt only by instruments. IV feels like traffic passing. The result of an earthquake with an intensity of IX is serious damage to buildings. XII earthquakes cause total destruction of manmade objects. The Mercalli scale of intensity is contrast to the Richter scale, which measures magnitude.

Isoseism A line on a map that joins areas that experience the same intensity of an earthquake. Such lines are usually concentric around the epicentre of the earthquake, with the strongest intensities towards the centre.

L wave In an earthquake, the part of the earthquake's vibration that travels over the surface of the earth and causes the damage.

Liquefaction The process in which a solid, such as soil or sand, acts like a liquid when it is shaken. This happens because the individual grains roll over one another.

Magnitude In an earthquake, the measure of the total energy released by the earthquake. It is measured on the Richter scale, which runs from zero upwards. The greatest value recorded is about 9. Each point on the scale represents a ten-fold increase on the point below.

An earthquake that measures 5 on the Richter scale releases ten times as much energy as an earthquake that measures 4. Unlike the Mercalli scale that measures intensity, each earthquake has only a single value of magnitude.

Observatory A scientific station that monitors natural events and processes. There are astronomical observatories that study the stars, and seismic observatories that keep and eye on earthquakes.

P wave In an earthquake, the part of an earthquake's vibration that radiates most quickly from the earthquake's focus. The P stands for primary, but it can also stand for pressure or push, as it travels by pushing at the rocks ahead of it.

Peninsula A body of land that is surrounded by sea on three sides.

Plate A section of the outermost part of the earth's structure. The outside of the earth is made up of less than a dozen plates. Where plates meet, moving in different directions, earthquakes and volcanoes occur.

Primary fissure The crack in the ground that marks the main movement that has produced a earthquake. The movement usually takes place along a fault, and the primary fissure marks the line of the fault.

Research Scientific investigation to discover facts.

Resonance When two pendulums are swinging, if they are swinging at exactly the same rate they are said to be in resonance.

Rift valley A valley formed as an area of land settles along a fault, or between two parallel faults. The movements may be due to earthquakes caused by the land pulling apart because of the movements of the plates.

Ring of Fire A region of volcanoes and earthquakes that surrounds the Pacific Ocean. It marks the edges of the earth's plates that form the ocean and the surrounding continents.

S wave In an earthquake, the part of an earthquake's vibration that radiates from the earthquake's focus just behind the P wave. The S stands for secondary, but it can also stand for shake, as it travels by shaking the rocks from side to side.

Satellite An instrument in orbit around the earth. It may carry sensors for examining the ground surface immediately below, communications devices for sending messages, or both.

Sediment Material, such as sand, silt, or mud, that is deposited by a river or on the bottom the sea.

Seismograph An instrument that detects earthquakes and prints out or displays a reading.

Seismologist A scientist who studies earthquakes. The study of earthquakes is called seismology.

Tsunami A giant sea wave produced by an underwater earthquake. It is sometimes called a tidal wave.

U.N.E.S.C.O. The United Nations Education Science and Cultural Organization. The organization of the United Nations that encourages the exchange of the these between different peoples.

INDEX